The Poetry of
FASHION DESIGN
A CELEBRATION OF THE WORLD'S MOST INTERESTING
Fashion Designers

Paz Diman

ROCKPORT

The Poetry of
FASHION DESIGN

A CELEBRATION OF THE WORLD'S MOST INTERESTING
Fashion Designers

Paz Diman

BEVERLY MASSACHUSETTS

ROCKPORT PUBLISHERS

Copyright © 2011 by **maomao** publications
First published in 2011 in the United States of America by
Rockport Publishers, a member of Quayside Publishing Group
100 Cummings Center
Suite 406-L
Beverly, MA 01915-6101
Telephone: (978) 282-9590
Fax: (978) 283-2742
www.rockpub.com

ISBN-13: 978-1-59253-715-0
ISBN-10: 1-59253-715-4

10 9 8 7 6 5 4 3 2 1

Publisher: Paco Asensio
Editorial coordination: Anja Llorella Oriol
Editor and texts: Paz Diman
Art director: Emma Termes Parera
Layout: Maira Purman
English translation: Cillero & de Motta

Editorial Project:
maomao publications
Via Laietana, 32 4th fl. of. 104
08003 Barcelona, España
Tel.: +34 93 268 80 88
Fax: +34 93 317 42 08
www.maomaopublications.com

Printed in China by 1010 Printing International Ltd

"Eat, drink, swallow my letter, carry it, transport it in you, like the law of a writing become your body (...)." Jacques Derrida

In *The Fashion System*, the French semiotician Roland Barthes envisioned a three-pillar structure that served to explain this phenomenon that is so elusive and difficult to characterize. Barthes says there is always "image-clothing," captured in the photography, then a "written-garment," which responds to its description in words, and "real-clothing," which is the design that exists beyond the lighting of the photography, fashion design, the pose of the model and the language that builds it with words.

Years later, this structural thinking was transformed with postmodernism. It was then, when Jacques Derrida proposed the deconstruction, disarming our images and beliefs and uncovering the metaphorical constructions accumulated within the concept.

One of the writings of this second thinker is entitled "Che cos'è poetry?" And in it Derrida describes poetry as a hedgehog that may seem helpless but, on the alert, it is really powerful. Similarly, the poetic construction shows its different meanings. The hedgehog's spines, whose tips point to the infinite, are like the power of words that flow through the heart, intimidate us and move us.

Today, the fashion industry moves between these two universes. Barthes' pillars put us in front of an industry that sometimes may seem frivolous, and the description of Derrida's poetry brings us closer to the private worlds of the creators. In between lies the body, the support. Clothing covers the certainty that we exist through a perfect machine wrapped in skin, in flesh.

The designers use the language, the stories they imagine for each collection as a starting point and a practical ability to create life through patterns, seams and fabric. Playing with the meaning of words (*feminine, ethereal, androgynous, magic, beauty*) is implicit in the garments through which the designers speak to us about their feelings, in an eternal battle between industry, trends, art and creation.

This book is a selection of individual worlds, the work of those designers who do not create fashion, but poems that clothe the body, sometimes changing it and subverting its shape. Gudrun & Gudrun's universe of delicate wool, Heidi Ackerman's three-dimensional sculptures, Bóas Kristjánsson and George Bezhanishvili's unintentional strength, color, and youth, Barbara í Gongini's commitment, Alejandra Quesada's fragile delicacy, the incomparable Walter Van Beirendonck's loyalty to such an individual vision, who, in fact, uses the slogan "Skin Poets Unite" in his Read My Skin collection... And these are only a handful of names of those who are not resigned to be restricted by the market's limitations, but play, imagine and create simply because they cannot stop.

The transgression of the volume, the perfection of the patterns, the beauty of what you cannot categorize, the strength of the poetry of fashion hastily infiltrates the pages of this book.

Fashion Designers

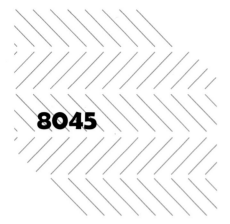

8045

www.kristjansson-boas.com

Bóas Kristjánsson is the Icelandic designer who gave life to 8045. He studied at the Academy of Arts in his native country and in Antwerp. His work is the result of different elements that come together in the world of fashion, from modeling and styling to photography and illustration.

His collections explore the color and the creative process, in which a garment emerges from the previous piece, linking each design in a generational chain. In his luxury sportswear collections, knitwear and radical cuts go hand in hand that draw inspiration from futuristic concepts.

Kristjánsson has presented his clothes in the men's fashion week in Paris and continues to explore the possibilities of fashion and collaborations with other disciplines from his homeland.

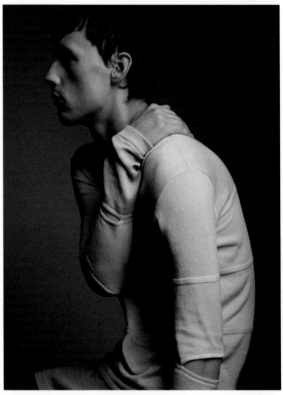

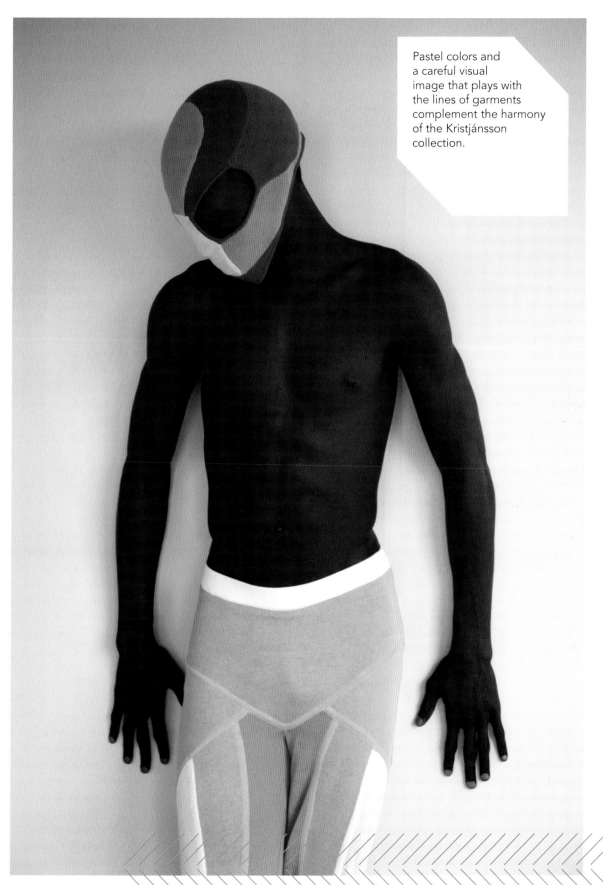

Pastel colors and a careful visual image that plays with the lines of garments complement the harmony of the Kristjánsson collection.

What is your favorite work of art?

I generally don't like art. I think it is an exercise in futility. Our generation cannot be impressed. However there are many artists who I like for their moods and aesthetics.

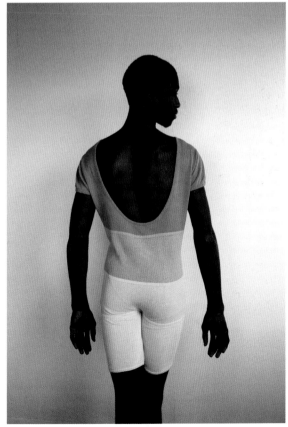

What is your fetish item of clothing, the one that we see time and time again in your collections?

Well, this question doesn't really apply to my work since I'm only working on my third collection and the previous ones have been only a few pieces. Knitted leggings are definitely my go-to garment though. I haven't really worn pants for a year now! They accomplish the silhouette that I'm trying to promote and they're just damned comfortable. You will see them in future collections without doubt. Not sure I will ever have a true leitmotif, I'd like to have the creative freedom to overturn my repertoire of garments between collections. We'll see...

Aldo Lanzini

Labeling the work of Aldo Lanzini is a complicated task. Combining design, fashion and art, the designer is an ace with the crochet hook, which he uses to create garments, toys and masks that are independently based on good humor. In his pieces the main concept is the creative process without knowing the end result: almost like a schizophrenic grandmother who cannot stop knitting.

Aldo Lanzini has captivated the world of fashion – Vogue has included him among the new up-and-coming designers to watch – as well as the world of art, presenting his unique work in several exhibitions.

Theatricality and skill at the service of the needle that never ceases to amaze: the latest crochet revolution born in Italy.

www.aldolanzini.eu

A toy, a prop or a work of art: the masks by Aldo Lanzini come alive, trapping the wearer and captivating the observer.

What is your favorite work of art?

A Yoko Ono work entitled *YES*.

What is your fetish item of clothing, the one that we see time and time again in your collections?

The one still to come!

Alejandra Quesada

The delicate and feminine universe of Alejandra Quesada was gradually developed while studying at ESMOD in Paris, in Central Saint Martins in London and her work experience with Isabel Marant, Tata-Naka and Alexander McQueen. At Alexander McQueen, Quesada was in charge of developing digital printing and textile design, which later would became a major trait in her work, characterised by embroidery and exquisite combination of different patterns.

The designer founded her own label in 2006 and has since presented her collections at fashion weeks in London, Paris and Mexico, her hometown. In addition to being curator, Quesada has dressed artists including Natalia Lafourcade, Julieta Venegas and Florence and the Machine.

www.alejandraquesada.com

© Marion Sosa

In her workshop, Quesada designs and makes her garment, from sketching the illustration and the selection of fabrics to carrying out the embroidery.

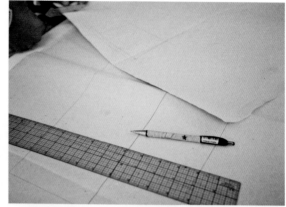

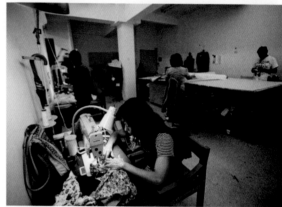
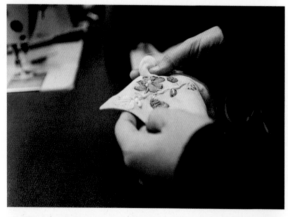

What is your favorite work of art?

I have many but I love the paintings by
Henry Darger.

Photos by Marion Sosa

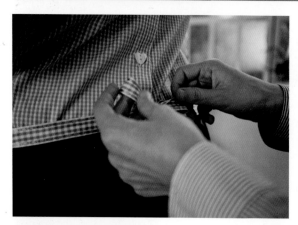

The embroidery work shows the influence of Mexican traditions in the work of the designer.

Photos by Gemma Booth

What is your fetish item of clothing, the one that we see time and time again in your collections?

Printed leggings. They always work!

Photos by Gemma Booth

Quesada's designs often share a common trait beyond the differences between the collections: the delicate view of femininity.

Andrea Cammarosano

andreacammarosano.com

© Eric De Mildt

Currently residing in Vienna, Andrea Cammarosano was born in Trieste (Italy). After completing his studies at the University of Florence and at Polimoda also in Florence, Cammarosano moved to Belgium to continue his education at the Royal Academy of Antwerp.

As an assistant to Walter van Beirendonk, the designer was fueled by a unique perspective of the world of fashion, where clothes are not merely an object but a personal mission statement. His collections, a combination of humor and expertise, provoked surprise for their surrealist hidden messages.

Cammarosano has exhibited his pieces in the Netherlands, Belgium, Austria, Germany and the United States and has collaborated with artists such as Fischerspooner, Ronald Stoops and Chantal Yzermans.

© Ronald Stoops

Fetishism that overwhelms with furious patterns and colors. In this collection, Cammarosano transgresses his previous collections.

© Ronald Stoops

Photos by Ronald Stoops

What is your favorite work of art?

It's a hard question, but I would say I like art when it crosses over with other disciplines. I think in this way it is communicated better, somehow in the same way as it happens with good fashion. In this sense I would choose a dish by Ferran Adrià, or Patrick Blanc's vertical garden at the Musée du Quai Branly in Paris. If you want something more classical, I've always liked very much the neon writing by Mario Merz at Venice's Guggenheim, or his Fibonacci numbers on the Mole Antonelliana in Turin.

Photos by Ronald Stoops

What is your fetish item of clothing, the one that we see time and time again in your collections?

Each collection has got one, but I guess I have a fetish for sculptural clothes and chunky shapes. I have a tendency to design men's garments with a certain volume on the front.

Andrea Llosa

After finishing her studies in business administration, the Peruvian Andrea Llosa moved to Barcelona, where she studied fashion design at the Escola Superior de Disseny i Moda Felicidad Duce. Llosa began her career in the cosmetics industry, working as brand manager for Unique-Yanbal in Lima and then as a freelancer in Myrurgia in Barcelona.

Her leap into the world of fashion was with Inditex, as a brand manager for Oysho. Thereafter, and until today, she has gradually built her career between her native Peru and Barcelona, working in the fashion industry with different responsibilities: costume designer for the movies *Madeinusa* and *La Teta Asustada*, assistant stylist at Rita Clip! Productions and designer for Sita Murt.

Combining the folkloric and urban style, all garments are made in Peru, where they work along with an artisan.

What is your favorite work of art?

Its difficult to choose one, but two of my
favorites are *False Idol*, by Damien Hirst,
and *Concert for Anarchy*, by Rebecca
Horn.

What is your fetish item of clothing, the one that we see time and time again in your collections?

A fully embroidered dress I designed for my first spring/summer 2009 collection, it took almost sixteen hours of embroidery. I made it three years ago and it still looks as good as new. I love it and I have in my closet as a major milestone in my career, not only for the work that I put into it, but because it was one of the garments in my first solo runway show at Fashion Week in Barcelona. Above all the international model Irina Lazareanu wore it, I could not believe it when I saw her wear it. I will never forget that moment.

Antonio Azzuolo

The Canadian designer Antonio Azzuolo graduated from Ryerson University in Toronto, specializing in men's tailoring. After completing his studies he moved to Milan, where he prepared himself to participate in the Hyères Young Designers Fashion show in the menswear category. In this contest, he won the first prize, opening the door for him to settle in Paris to launch his career.

Before founding a.a, his own label, Azzuolo worked in the workshops of two institutions in the fashion industry: Hermès and Kenzo. He also worked as design director for the Purple and Black labels by Ralph Lauren.

His diverse experience within the sector is reflected in his garments, which mix casual and elegant design with luxury and glamour.

antonioazzuolo.com

The fifth collection by a.a, fall/winter 2010, plays with the image of the cowboy, updating it and giving it an interesting urban-chic style.

What is your favorite work of art?

Not one favorite work of art... Too difficult to choose!

What is your fetish item of clothing, the one that we see time and time again in your collections?

Hand tailored DB jacket with leather silver trim and a driver!

Barbara í Gongini

www.barbaraigongini.dk

Committed to sustainability, art and design, Barbara í Gongini is the eponymous label of this designer born in the Faroe Islands, between Scotland and Iceland. Gongini graduated from the Institute of Unica Design in Denmark, and since then has created two distinct lines: Barbara í Gongini, her most creative and experimental facet, and The Black Line, which simplifies the former line into more basic garments.

Her androgynous and futuristic collections are proof that sustainability is not incompatible with style, as each material is selected according to environmentally friendly criteria. Defined geometric cuts and the importance of the versatility of the garments means that they can adapt to the personality of the wearer.

From a conceptual perspective, the design approach is a key to understanding the work of Barbara í Gongini.

Photos by veerasawmy.com

Photos by Nicky De Silva

What is your favorite work of art?

Ceiling Painting (YES Painting), by Yoko Ono, 1966.

The design challenges the complexity in the process of making clothes. The final form of the design reflects the experimentation in its creation.

What is your fetish item of clothing, the one that we see time and time again in your collections?

My sustainable plastic knitted dress from autumn/winter 2010.

Photos by veerasawmy.com

Bibian Blue

www.bibianblue.com

Combining alternative fashion and theater, Bibian Blue is the quintessential Spanish designer in the universe of all that is retro, vintage and burlesque.

The lines of the label are diverse, moving between sobriety, elegance and more radical and nonconformist creations. Still, the key is always the same: enhancing the female figure and the use sophisticated fabrics, such as the corset, by itself or in a dress.

Passionate about fashion, currently she has over fifty different patterns that are inspired by different eras. Her references are the different avant-garde artistic concepts as well as haute couture, the pop and retro scene, music, comics and vintage wardrobe.

Meticulous details are essential to create the sensation of the characteristic voluptuousness of Bibian Blue's work.

What is your favorite work of art?

Any work by Waterhouse and the Pre-Raphaelites, although I am also a big fan of pop surrealism. Artists such as Mark Ryden, Ray Caesar and Nathalie Shau, to name a few. In photography I'd definitely say Recuenco, and in fashion, the list, to be honest, is quite long, but I love Galliano, McQueen and Mugler.

What is your fetish item of clothing, the one that we see time and time again in your collections?

Corsets, of course!.

c.neeon

C.neeon is a combination of the childhood nicknames of Clara Leskovar and Doreen Schulz, the designers behind this particular German label created in 2004. It was that year when they both decided to join forces to present a collection at the International Festival of Hyères. They won the "Grand Prix" and this forced them to kick start their career in fashion. Next, they presented collections at London Fashion Week, they exhibited their garments in the German Museum of Decorative Art, they designed a collection for Topshop and in 2006 they received a Baltic Fashion Award.

Their collections are characterized by striking graphic prints and they create silhouettes with intriguing asymmetrical cuts and architectural volumes. The designers draw inspiration from their home, Berlin, and C.neeon attempts to reflect the city's multifaceted energetic character in their creations.

The Flamingos collection is inspired by the image of these animals, using a pastel color as a base and imitating the shape of the wings in the cuts.

What is your favorite work of art?

At the moment we love both the work of Hannah Hoech. Our spring/summer 2011 collection is inspired by her fantastic collages.

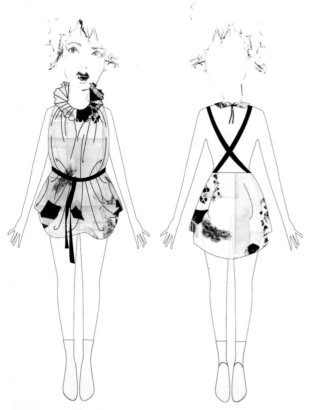

Inspired by images from the artist Hannah Hoech, the silhouettes of the Boa Perlina collection are presented as the silhouettes of magical flowery creatures.

**What is your fetish item of clothing,
the one that we see time and time
again in your collections?**

The dress Coque du village is our
favorite piece of the winter collection
2010/11.

Capara

www.capara.be

Founded in 2009, Capara is the label and the surname of the sisters Vera and Olivera. Born in Sarajevo, the Capara sisters were brought up in Germany and they moved to Belgium to study fashion in the Royal Academy of Fine Art. As a team, and also separately, the designers worked in studios such as Dries Van Noten, Delvaux, Raf Simons and Maison Martin Margiela, where they developed one of their lines of craftsmanship.

Today, Capara develops a visual language that is not only limited to garments, but also includes furniture, objects and art, working along with other artists. Behind their collections is the analysis of various anthropological subjects, inspired by literature, poetry and the progress of a constantly changing world.

© Johan Sandberg

© Mike Steegmans

The tones of
the Indifference
collection reveal its
nature-inspired theme.
The wood and sand result
in a brown palette.

What is your favorite work of art?

Gerhard Richter's Baader Meinhof series, 1988.

Wonderful Life
plays with the
symmetries and
dualities, and links
different elements that
create unity in the entire
design.

Photos by Johan Sandberg

The Poetry of Fashion Design 73

What is your fetish item of clothing, the one that we see time and time again in your collections?

Autumn/winter collection Wonderful Life, silhouette 5.

Photos by Mike Steegmans

Dassios

www.dassios.com

This lover of art and aesthetics managed to channel his artistic passion toward jewelry and accessory design. Gradually, the project evolved to have several different lines, which all share an admiration for craftsmanship and detail.

Linking different cultural traditions, Dassios brings together art and techniques characterizing far-flung points on the globe. Afghanistan embroidery, silks manufactured in India, Samarkand velvet and leather from Morocco are just some of the materials combined in an interesting collection. The results are unique, unrepeatable artworks that reinterpret traditional costumes from a modern perspective.

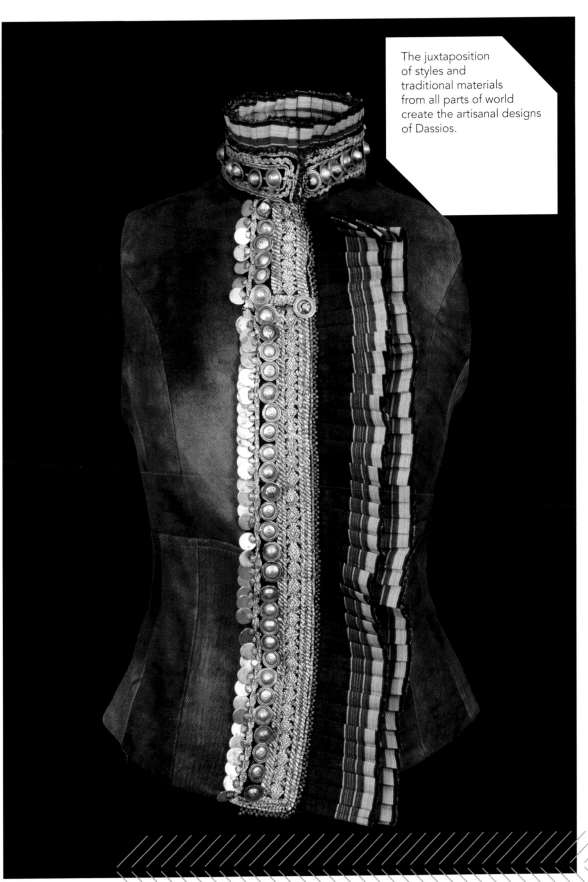

The juxtaposition of styles and traditional materials from all parts of world create the artisanal designs of Dassios.

What is your favorite work of art?

Having a passionate interest in decorative and fine arts, Dassios found in fashion design the perfect expression of his artistic nature and aesthetic principles. Painting, sculpture, music and dancing are some of the arts that are integral to the Dassios culture, but if one and only art field is to be selected, that would be music as the designer's most favorite.

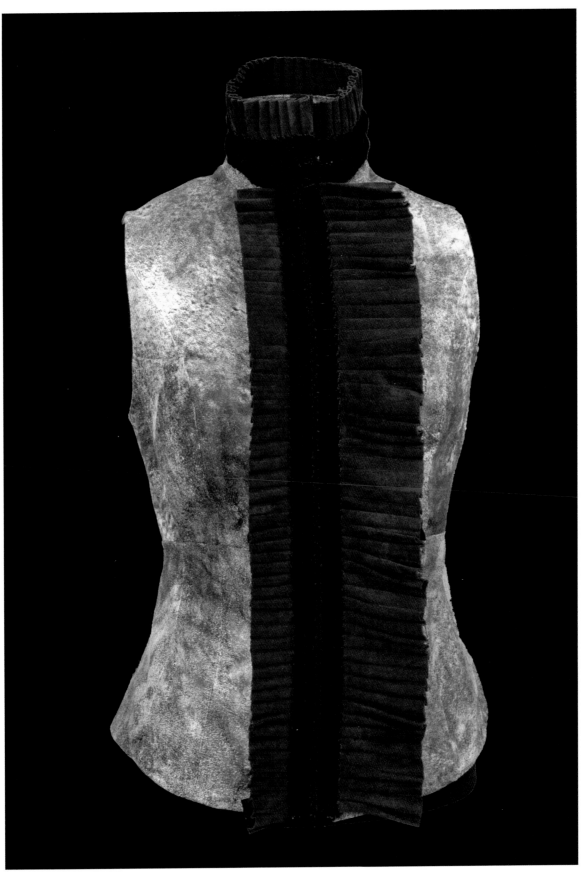

What is your fetish item of clothing, the one that we see time and time again in your collections?

As a matter of fact, there is no certain design that could be described as a go-to and be followed on every collection. Because every collection has to be unique in terms of designs and in line to the Dassios characteristic work. On the other hand, if someone looks the Dassios collections carefully they may easily understand that the pleated fabrics as a technique is a kind of trademark way that is followed in every collection by the designer either in jewelery or in other fashion designs. Pleated fabrics can be seen in various aspects of the Dassios designs as, for example, in collars, manchettes, sleeves, or even in his jewelery designs as a kind of pattern.

Deryck Walker

The Scot Deryck Walker studied fashion in Cardonald Glasgow College before moving to London. In London, he worked for the Boudicca and as an assistant for Robert Carey-Williams, then he moved to Milan and landed a job at Versace. His first menswear collection was launched in 2005 and sold at the prestigious Dover Street Market. Three years later, he designed his first female collection.

Walker's style is based on anachronistic elegance, which combines classical elements with modern details, resulting in a recognizable personal style. Awarded Scottish fashion designer at the Scottish Style Awards in 2008 and 2009, Walker has been working with Topman, John Smedley, Harris Tweed, Holland and Sherry.

www.deryckwalker.net

© David Eustace www.davideustace.com

The designer's
work converges in
the meeting point of
more traditional patterns
and a more modern stamp.

What is your favorite work of art?

*Three Studies for Figures at the Base of
a Crucifixion* (second edition, 1944), by
Francis Bacon.

What is your fetish item of clothing, the one that we see time and time again in your collections?

I think it would be one of my razor-tailored suits as they are very seductive without being overt!

Dino Alves

www.dinoalves.eu

The *enfant terrible* of Portuguese fashion was born in Arcos in 1967. After studying painting at the Escola Superior Artistica do Porto and taking a course in professional photography in the INEF, he spent a brief period at the Portuguese Cinémathèque, until he presented his first collection in 1994. Since then, he has worked as a set dresser, stylist and designer, participating in several plays, advertising campaigns, fashion editorials and exhibitions.

His collections were presented in various European countries, and he is a designer who never misses the Lisbon fashion week. His provocative and dramatic style expresses the many disciplines covered in his work, making Dino an indispensable personality in the fashion world.

© Gonçalo Gaioso

Ficha Técnica

Dino Alves atelier

Vestido peça 14

Desenho plano

The relaxed
but perfectionist
style of Alves can be
seen in the sketches:
loose lines and polished
technique.

What is your favorite work of art?

It's difficult to choose a work of art as my favorite. It depends on the different decades, different mediums of expression and the artistic movements. In every one I have something that I like. Recently I prefer the installation pieces, photography and video art. Since the beginning of the twentieth century and the modern art there are lots of artist that I appreciate, such as Henry Matisse, Egon Schiele, William de Kooning, Gerhard Richter, Marcel Duchamp, Joseph Beuys, Joel Peter Witkin, Basquiat, Jeff Koons, Vik Muniz, Damien Hirst, Cindy Sherman, Bill Viola, Julian Opie and many others.

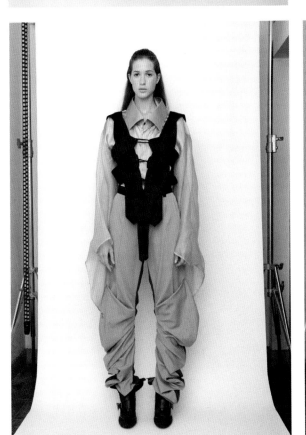

What is your fetish item of clothing, the one that we see time and time again in your collections?

It depends on the different periods of my career. At the beginning, for example, I always used some recycled pieces that I customized to include in the collections. I think the pants I do, mainly from the winter 2002/03 collection, when I only did pants as the concept of the show, I developed a nice pattern and from that moment I always do some and they fit in a nice way especially in the man's body. But the idea I have been repeating lately is the use of different and unexpected material to do some kind of garment. Crochet and tricot techniques with leather wire or plastics or other yarn made with other kind of fabrics, for example.

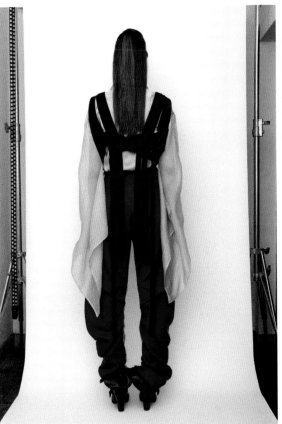

Photos by Rui Vasco/Archivo MODALISBOA

Playing with
the concept of
transgender, the fall/
winter 2010/11 collection
was presented with male
models, a declaration of
intent.

Dora Abodi

Coming from a family of artists, Dora Abodi was born in Cluj-Napoca (Romania). After graduating as a lawyer and studying journalism, the designer decided to make a leap into the world of fashion, studying at Mod'Art International School in Budapest.

Her own label, established in her final year, was a complete explosion of creativity. Clothing, accessories, handbags, each one of her designs showed a very personal skill that had always been latent. A fusion of luxury and experimentation, her clothes are incredibly chic and all materials are environmentally friendly. Named Woman of the Year in 2010 by *Glamour* magazine, her designs have captivated the international press and started to sell worldwide.

Music, comics, literature, contemporary art, science fiction... All these influences converge in the work of Abodi.

The fantasy world depicted in this collection is achieved through the use of metallic fabrics and through appliqués on the clothes.

© Balint Trunkó

What is your favorite work of art?

My parents and my grandfather are painters and fine artists so I love their paintings and other art works. It's hard to choose one art piece, as there are many paintings, sculptures, buildings, movies, novels, music, fashion designs that I really love. Some examples: Dürer, Vermeer, Michelangelo, Jeff Koons; architects like Wright, John Lautner and Lajos Kozma or Gaudí; writers like Poe, Updike, Lawrence, Durrell, Gibson, Proust, Capote, Gyula Krúdy; or designers like Chanel, Chalayan, Prada or Balenciaga.

Photos by Jon Moe

What is your fetish item of clothing, the one that we see time and time again in your collections?

My nude dresses with huge shoulders from the spring/summer 2010 collection, the asymmetric heart-shaped bags, the fade lilac bag with stuffed beans and huge fringes and the iridescent green jacket from the fall/ winter 2011. Of course there are many other favorite pieces, the pleated black maxi bag, the small envelope bags in a lot of colors and versions...

El Delgado Buil

Anna Figuera Delgado and Macarena Ramos Buil met at the Escola Superior de Disseny in Sabadell. After completing their studies in 2004, they created their own company and label, El Delgado Buil. Since then, they have presented their collections in the Barcelona and Lisbon edition of Circuit, the Cibeles Runway shows and fashion weeks in Lithuania and Mexico.

They have been awarded the "Grand Prix" from Marie Claire fashion and have won for two consecutive years the L'Oréal Award for the best collection by a new designer. They have also collaborated with several brands, including Sony PlayStation, Kipling, Lladró and Showstudio. Since March 2007, El Delgado Buil has its own store/workshop in the Gothic Quarter of Barcelona, and their clothes are sold in France, Germany, Denmark, Australia and Japan.

www.eldelgadobuil.com

© César Segarra

The images on this page show a collaboration of the designers of the label Scorpion, a proposal marked by the beauty of the ethereal.

What is your favorite work of art?

There are many such as *Soir Bleur*, by
Edward Hopper, or the photographs
by Diane Arbus or Ed Templeton and
the exhibition by Yves Saint Laurent
in the Petit Palais.

What is your fetish item of clothing, the one that we see time and time again in your collections?

Again there are many, but from the latest collection, Joiner Creek, we are especially fond of the fur garments, knitwear and Kalgan lamb necks.

The Joiner Creek collection combines fur, vintage prints and tartans, as well as different materials such as leather, cashmere and wool.

Femme Maison

g.bezhanishvili@gmail.com
franziskafuerpass@gmail.com

Franziska Fürpass and George Bezhanishvili are members of the playground that is Femme Maison, both graduates of the University of Applied Arts in Vienna. Their long friendship evolved into a professional collaboration, and so the collective universe of Femme Maison emerged.

A combination of sculpture and fashion, their proposal arose from collage, where volumes and different materials create intimist pieces. Their designs, which are like a work of art, invite reflection, provoking the imagination to discover the secret behind their work. Bleached upholstery, drapery and recycled leather are elements they combine to protect the body, covering it in a deep and fraternal way.

© Sia Kermani

The first collection by Femme Maison is inspired by the work of the artist Louise Bourgeois, based on emotional relationships and context.

What is your favorite work of art?

The Secret, by Auguste Rodin.

What is your fetish item of clothing, the one that we see time and time again in your collections?

Rose ruffled dress.

The designs by Femme Maison are intimate and complex, creating real three-dimensional sculptures that envelop the body.

Friederike von Wedel-Parlow

www.vonwedelparlow.com

Born in Berlin, Friederike von Wedel-Parlow studied fashion with Vivienne Westwood at the University of Arts in his hometown. After graduating he stayed on in the center as a lecturer, and during that time he founded the label Von Wedel & Tiedeken with Regina Tiedeken. The unusual cuts and designer's innate interest in storytelling led to fantastic collections, plus several television and film collaborations.

In 2008, along with Volkswagen Group in China, Von Wedel-Parlow took his first step towards sustainable fashion, designing bags with solar panels that served as chargers for mobile phones or MP3 players. His interest in the environment led him to create his first individual collection, Project No. 1, which is based on the use of recycled and organic cotton fabrics.

The collection is characterized by the use of all of the cloth. Thus, a jersey cut in a loop becomes a fringed poncho.

What is your favorite work of art?

Zilvinas Kempina's *Flying Tape*, Michael Heizer's *Earthworks*, Pippilotti Rist's *Ever is all over*.

Photos by Özgür Albayrak

What is your fetish item of clothing, the one that we see time and time again in your collections?

There are two: one is a patchwork-system to build a shoulder part out of rectangles or o-shapes, that I developed for my diploma collection and came back to it on essential occasions. It is kind of a dramatic thing in very different versions. The other is more silent, a simple pattern system for a dress called E-squaredress. It's basically a piece of fabric formed out of two half circles, which is matched in the back with the help of a big rectangular gusset.

Von Wedel-Parlow's inspiration comes from the images of the urban Amazons by the Berlin artist Jen Ray.

Gareth Moody

www.chroniclesofnever.com

© Scott Lowe

Gareth Moody, a member of the trio of bad guys who created the Australian label Tsubi, found his own unique creative world with his solo project, Chronicles of Never. What began as a line of accessories and footwear led to complete collections, in which a subtle common denominator can be identified: the understated perception of the passage of time.

Moody's space is gentle, almost ethereal. His clothes are characterized by the flow of materials, allowing the textiles to acquire their own personality when they are worn. Reverie goes hand in hand with comfort, a key point in all the stories that inspire their collections. Between fantasy, surrealism and magic, Chronicles of Never is as an exquisite personal vision that transcends the tyranny of fashion.

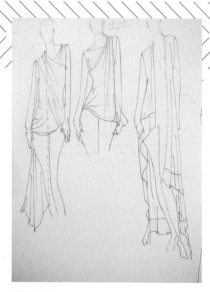

The designer's style, defined as "pagan tailoring," evokes the mysticism of the fantasy stories which characterize his collections.

What is your favorite work of art?

To be honest I have struggled with this question. Providing on favorite work of art—that's an impossibility for me. So I'm going with *The Last Whole Earth Catalog*, an amazing guidebook to life, not a work of art in the traditional sense but art nonetheless.

Working with the
materials makes the
clothes look worn, like
a kind of second skin that
adapts to the figure.

What is your fetish item of clothing, the one that we see time and time again in your collections?

I tend to get the most enjoyment out of outerwear, for the most part leather. It's so tactile.

George Bezhanishvili

This Georgian designer is very clear about what is the source of his inspiration: himself. His collections, always fun with a slight touch of irony, arise from a personal perspective on the world.

A disciple of Veronique Branquinho and Bernhard Willhelm, Bezhanishvili studied at the University of Applied Arts in Vienna and worked at Fabrics Interseason. He also has been recognized with several awards, including the Swiss Textile Prize 2008.

George Bezhanishvili, thinking about both the past and present, creates the future, presenting his work as an intimate diary. The details of daily life, music and the people of his adoptive city, Vienna, work as a collection of epiphanies that are reflected in his designs.

www.notjustalabel.com/george_bezhanishvili

© Lukas White Gansterer

Outfit

In his artwork, the designer composes the overall look of the figure, including the accessories and testing the fabrics used to construct them.

Photos by Andreas Waldschuetz

What is your favorite work of art?

Study for a Self-Portrait—Triptych, by Francis Bacon.

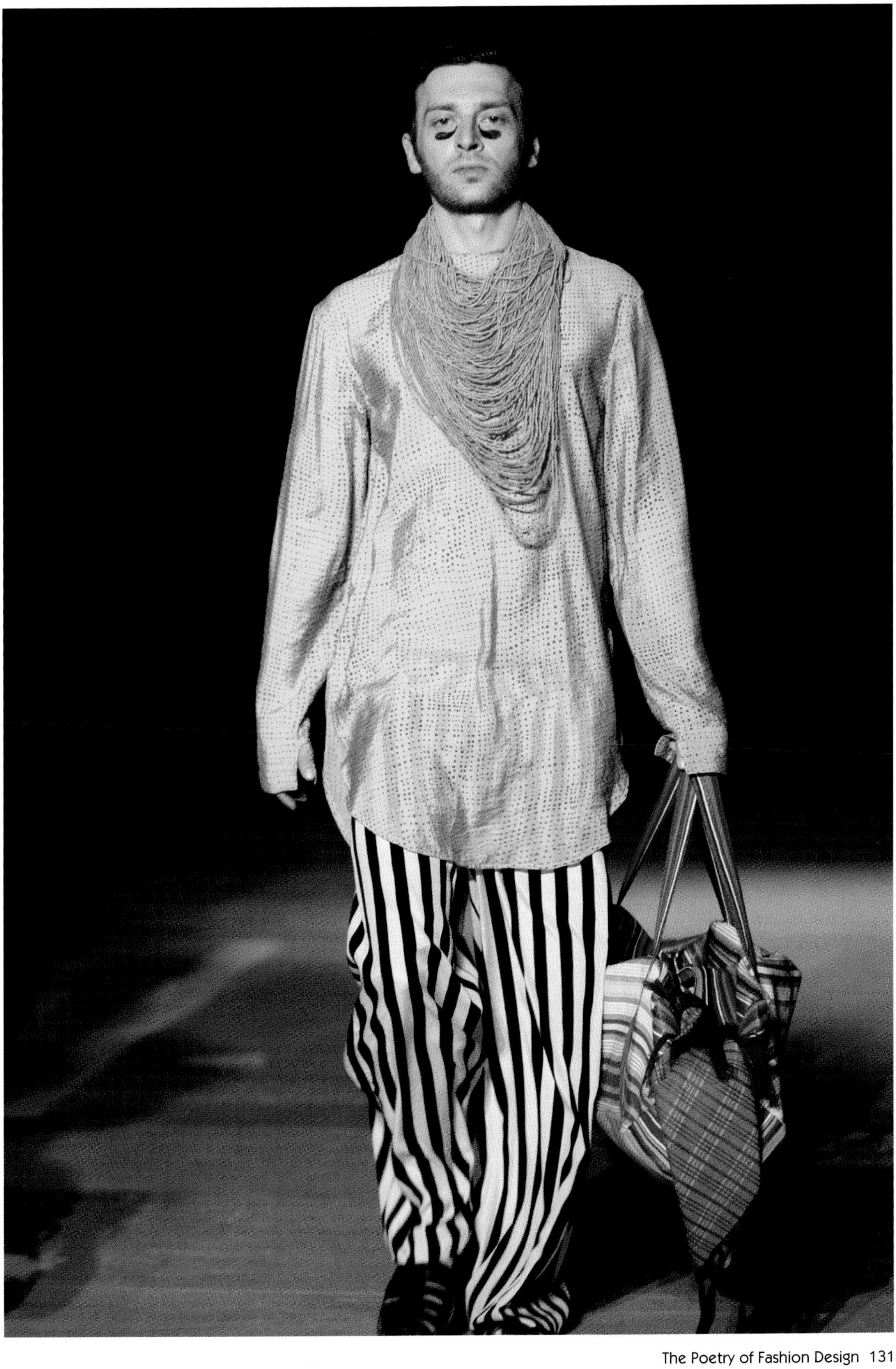

© Andreas Waldschuetz

Gauze fabrics
are the perfect
counterpoint to
the vibrant colors that
Bezhanishvili chooses to
create the image of an
Indian prince.

Photos by Andreas Waldschuetz

What is your fetish item of clothing, the one that we see time and time again in your collections?

Men's mohair dress-coat.

Gudrun & Gudrun

Experts in knitwear, the two designers Gudrun & Gudrun were born on the Faroe Islands, a small archipelago in the North Atlantic. With only 45,000 inhabitants, its calm and tranquil setting, with its own language and culture, and its natural isolation is the inspiration for their collections.

   Their designs, apart from knitwear including garments made from cotton and footwear, are made by hand. However, their delicacy does not detract from their personality: Gudrun & Gudrun's objective is to put mohair on a par with leather, even when they should provoke completely different sensations. That is where their ability to manage their own language, a unique universe lies.

Miracle-workers
of knitted fabrics,
the designers manage
to build forms that seem
impossible with these
materials.

What is your favorite work of art?

I could mention a lot of pieces and a lot of artists. But what always catches my attention is simplicity. Art made simple. It can be compared with the way we work with our collection—it can be scary to be silent. To make something simple, but still very strong—you feel naked. At the moment I am very fascinated by the Dutch flower artist Wouter Dolk and also Faroese Rannvá Kunoy.

What is your fetish item of clothing, the one that we see time and time again in your collections?

Our star sweater is new and iconic and there is no collection without the stars. The fit is perfect and it is made very simply. It has been the best seller for five years and it's a favorite in all markets. This winter we made a woolen dress with the stars and in the newest spring/summer 2011 collection we have made a series in silk with woolen stars—all in the same champagne tone.

Heidi Ackerman

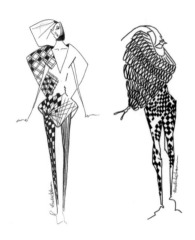

The collections by Heidi Ackerman combine cutting-edge style and sustainability. Using techniques that combine craftsmanship and technology, the designer creates unique textiles and prints using environmentally friendly materials such as cork. Her obsession with architecture, movement and the future is explored on the runway and in publications, and is embodied in her collections, which are sold in Toronto.

Her work has been recognized on numerous occasions and she has received the award for the emerging young designer at Fashion R4 2009. She has also collaborated with Opera Erratica, with the National Ballet of Canada, Lindsay Sinclair and Ndeur & Le Creative Sweatshop. Ackerman usually presents her collections at the Alternative Arts and Fashion Week in her native Toronto.

flightheidiackerman.blogspot.com

© X-Processed

Made in a monumental way, the designs transcend their purpose and function as garments and magnificent sculptures.

What is your favorite work of art?

I love the Dada, Surrealist and Constructivist movements of the early twentieth century. I'd have to say that Marcel Duchamp's *Nude Descending A Staircase* is one of my all-time favorite works of art. I love the way he uses fractured imagery to create movement.

Photos by X-Processed

Clash of contexts: accessories that look like they are straight from the set of *Metropolis* by Friz Lang along with patterns and clothing oozing color and modernity.

Photos by Sai Sivanesan

Linked to theater costumes, Acker-man designs clamor for a stage to fill with his impressive personality.

What is your fetish item of clothing, the one that we see time and time again in your collections?

In my work I explore architecture through cloth and the body. I find that I often repeat or expand upon techniques throughout my collections. One dress, which I call the Bow dress, has become a signature of my line and has helped to define it as a line that experiments with geometry and architecture. For me this dress has opened up new avenues of invention and interpretations of building garments, which has been influential on every season since.

Hilda Maha

www.hildamaha.com

Brought up in Italy but with Albanian origins Hilda Maha moved to London to pursue her passion for design. She launched her label in 2009, after completing her studies at Central Saint Martins and after spending a year as a print designer at Friulprint.

Now in Italy, Hilda creates her romantic designs with the finest fabrics and oozes the essence of the garment. With emphasis on highlighting the female form, the waist, shoulders and sleeves are key points in all her clothes.

Her line is identified by the use of striking colors and patterns, achieving a fresh, youthful design that is also timeless. Her knowledge of textiles is one of the key points of her collections.

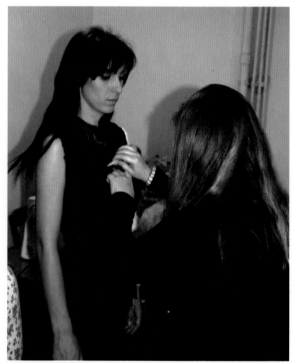

Skillful volumes, textures and prints are the three lines that prevail in the creation of the Maha's delicate feminine poetry.

What is your favorite work of art?

I love art, I always have, so there's a lot coming to mind with a question like this. What jumps in mind straight away is any work of the Pre-Raphaelite period, Dante Gabriel Rossetti, Sir Edward Coley, John William Waterhouse, *The Cave of the Storm Nymphs* by Sir Edward John Poynter and *Ulysses and the Sirens* by Herbert James Drapers; anything by Gustav Klimt, pieces like *Sea Serpents*, *Mermaids* and *The Kiss* come to mind; Vincent van Gogh's work, Monet's *Water Lilies*, *The Lacemaker* by Vermeer, the work of Ernst Ludwig Kirchner, *The Virgin of the Rocks* and sketches by Leonardo da Vinci and a couple of untitled works by J. M. Basquiat, but I could easily go on and on.

What is your fetish item of clothing, the one that we see time and time again in your collections?

I would say my flared coat with inserts. I have both repeated them and reworked them and taken inspiration from them. It's a kind of shape and fit I really like, and from any angle you watch it you will see something different. It's never boring, it's very flattering to the figure, quite dramatic but sharp and strong.

House of Diehl

www.houseofdiehl.com

Mary Jo Diehl and Roman Milisic form the creative team of House of Diehl. The label's groundbreaking work transcends the boundaries between fashion, art, music and performance, and expresses solemn declarations of intent expressed through its design and multimedia experiences.

House of Diehl has presented its creations in various places: with Sonic Youth and Rem Koolhaas in the Greenspace Festival in Spain, along with David Lachapele and Gwen Stefani in the Rich Girl video and with Elton John, Liza Minelli and Versace at the Life Ball that was held in the Rathaus in Vienna, and in various other exhibitions.

The collections have also been praised by critics, nominated for the Gen Art Styles Avant-garde Award, the Ecco Domani Fashion Foundation Award, and the Triumph International Fashion Award in 2004–2005.

(c)house of diehl

Graphic design, experimentation and pop culture: the perfect blend to decipher the aesthetic code of House of Diehl.

What is your favorite work of art?

MJ: Warhol's *Soup Can*, because it was a telescope into art's future.
RM: The Sphinx, because it took too long.

What is your fetish item of clothing, the one that we see time and time again in your collections?

MJ: There's nothing I love more than my first piece: Brand New Me. It proved to me something that I had only dreamed about till then. This piece is the fulcrum of HoD—philosophically, emotionally, aesthetically.
RM: My eyewear. Nothing teases like a look!

Ilaria Nistri

In 2006, Ilaria Nistri presented her first collection on the Paris Stock Exchange Trade. Success was almost instant, with her clothes being sold in international stores like Liberty in London, Lane Crawford in Hong Kong, and Mercury in Moscow. The beautiful fabrics and sensuousness of her designs have captivated the public.

Two years later, the designer was selected as one of the new emerging talents by the Italian edition of *Vogue*. She also reached the finals of the contest Who Is On Next?, organized by the prestigious magazine and Alta Roma.

Ilaria Nistri also presented her collections at Fashion Weeks in Milan and Tokyo. Embraced by the media in her country, the designer was selected again by *Vogue* for its Cahier des Talents in 2010.

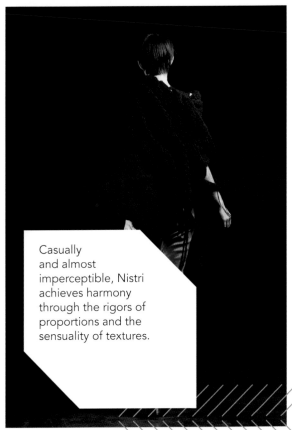

Casually and almost imperceptible, Nistri achieves harmony through the rigors of proportions and the sensuality of textures.

What is your favorite work of art?

The tomb of Ilaria del Carretto by the sculptor Jacopo Della Quercia dating from 1406–1408, which is preserved in the Cathedral of San Martino in Lucca. This is something I have a special attachment to because my name was given to me out of my mother's particular love for it. And then perhaps all thirteenth and fourteenth century Florentine art, which my family collects. I also feel great interest in contemporary art when it experiments with new languages for communication.

What is your fetish item of clothing, the one that we see time and time again in your collections?

Leather pants; they're a feature of all my collections. I always revisit and reinterpret them to suit the collection. They're always tight-fitting, with inserts in different fabric; they're the result of research and experimentation with cuts in the style of a female warrior, like the ones I've designed for my new spring/ summer 2011 collection.

Iris van Herpen

www.irisvanherpen.com

Since graduating from the ArtEZ School in her native Holland, Iris van Herpen has rapidly developed her ability to create visually stunning designs. Disciple of Alexander McQueen and Viktor & Rolf, Van Herpen tries to narrow the gap between fashion and technology from the experimental perspective of Hussein Chalayan.

Based in London, the designer created her label in 2007. In her work, volumes, folds and lace fuse together to create clothes that transcend the boundaries of fashion design, and are more similar to a garment-object, a work of art. At the moment, Van Herpen, committed to a futuristic line, is a born and bred transgressor who also has a relentless ability to reinterpret elements and materials.

The illustrations of the designer (opposite) are only the first step that leads to the creation of her stunning pieces.

Photos by Michel Zoeter

What is your favorite work of art?

I do not have one favorite work of art, there is too much that I like. But of course the work of artists that I know have more value for me, because I know more about the personality and reasons behind it. One of the most powerful forms of art is music. One special piece that is valuable for me is the music that Salvador Breed made for my last show at the Amsterdam Fashion Week. The magic of music is that it can bring you back in time. If I hear that piece of music, it brings me back to the process of making the collection, the exciting moment of the show itself and to the good people that were there. It brings the moment back to life better than any photo or painting.

Photos by Michel Zoeter

What is your fetish item of clothing, the one that we see time and time again in your collections?

Choosing a garment is difficult because it's changing all the time. But today I would say the rapid prototyping design from my latest collection. It looks as the bone structure of a non-existant animal.

The Synesthesia collection toys with empty volumes in an exquisite metamorphosis between the human body and skeleton of an insect.

Juan Antonio Ávalos

Juan Antonio Ávalos is a promising new Spanish fashion designer, who studied at Escola Superior de Disseny i Moda Felicidad Duce, in Barcelona. As a student, the designer was awarded the Tu Stilo, Tu Studio Award from L'Oréal Paris in Madrid.

His first collection was awarded the Emerging Designer Award in Catalunya in the first edition of 080 Barcelona Fashion, which catapulted him to Paris to study in 2008 with designer Bernard Willhelm and Thomas Engel Hart. A year later, the designer created his prêt-à-porter male namesake label.

Judged by the most demanding juries, Ávalos alternates the development of his own collections and collaborations with brands such as Nike, Converse and Superga, and photographers such as Björn Tagemose and Daniel Riera.

Mazinger Z is the inspiration for the fall/winter 2010/11 collection, the humor and nostalgia of a sonic Peter Pan in physical and rounded silhouettes.

What is your favorite work of art?

Composition VII, by Kandinsky.

What is your fetish item of clothing, the one that we see time and time again in your collections?

Majinga Zetto Replica Jacket, fall/winter 2010/11.

Karishma Shahani

www.karishmashahani.com

Recently graduated from the London College of Fashion Technology and Fashion Design, Karishma Shahani draws inspiration from her native India. Mimicking the skills of artisans, the designer creates intricate and exquisite handmade garments.

Her first steps in the world of fashion have been praised on sites like Vogue.co.uk, GraziaDaily.co.uk, and iD Magazine.com, and her designs have been present in exhibitions such as "Just Go Ethical Fabulous" and "Design Means Business." She has also been nominated for the London Design Festival and the Future Map.

Currently, the designer works with the artist Amy Sol in a non-profit, eco-friendly fashion project called Jhoole to improve the conditions of artisans from the rural state of Madhya Pradesh in India.

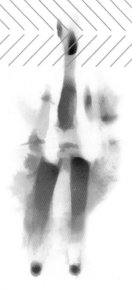

In the collection,
Yatra overlaps
fabrics and textures,
fusing different elements
that characterize the Indian
culture.

Photos by Sean Michael

What is your favorite work of art?

There are so many beautiful pieces of art that I adore. From van Gogh's *Blossoming Almond Tree* to Moscow's Cathedral of Intercession of Theotokos on the Moat—popularly known as St. Basil's Cathedral—to the Rabari community in Rann of Kutch, India always dressed as moving pieces of art, to Rajendra Shyam's Gond paintings, a tribal folk art.

The colors were taken from paintings depicting various Indian gods, recreated through natural methods of dyeing.

What is your fetish item of clothing, the one that we see time and time again in your collections?

The piece called Devta would be the leitmotif of my work as it was my starting point with all its color and texture. A close second would be Sada and the bags created out of blankets and embroidery.

Katie Eary

www.katieeary.co.uk

Katie Eary, the London-based designer, graduated from the Royal College of Art. She had barely left the college when one the first calls she received was from the British edition of *Vogue* magazine: Mario Testino wanted to shoot her pieces on Kate Moss, and her line was designed for men...

This was the starting point of a career that promises to be as meteoric as her explosive designs. Color and good humor are key elements in these collections as well as the forms that challenge any preconceived idea. Her clothes have the attitude to clamor for a definite change. Katie Eary uses wool, leather, metal and even Swarovski crystals to the service of transgression.

Inspired by the book *Marabou Stork Nightmares* by Irvine Welsh, the prints and cuts reflect the implicit aggressiveness in the narrative text.

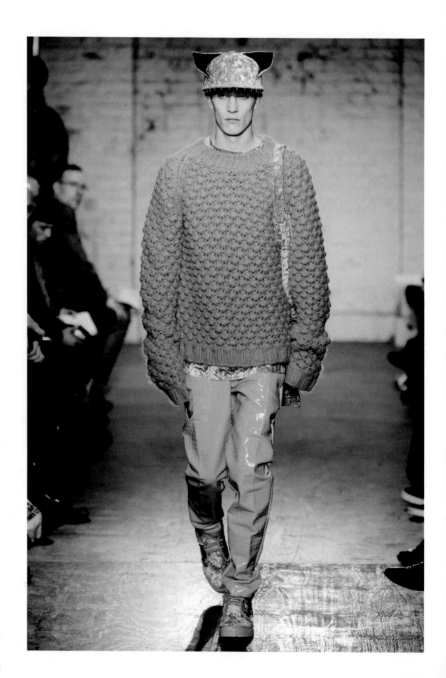

What is your favorite work of art?

All YBA (Young British Artists), Jake and Dinos Chapman—pretty much everything they touch. The book *Fucking Hell*. I love Tracey Emin, also, very, very much.

Wool, leather
and fur, mimicking
the shape of animals,
textures and explosive
colors bring us on a
hallucinatory journey.

What is your fetish item of clothing, the one that we see time and time again in your collections?

My favorite piece from the last collection was the full green snake look.

Khalid Al Qasimi

www.qasimi.com

After finishing his studies in French and Hispanic literature, Khalid Al Qasimi studied architecture at the Architectural Association and continued his education by enrolling in fashion at Central Saint Martins. In 2008 he launched his label, Qasimi.

The combination of his childhood memories in the Middle East and his passion for architecture are expressed in his well-structured and minimalist garments. His label is also characterized by modern tailoring and bold avant-garde forms. Jessica Alba, Lily Cole and Paloma Faith are among the artists who have worn clothes from his female line, Femme Qasimi.

Currently, the designer has decided to focus on his menswear collection, which he continues to present on the official runway shows in Paris Fashion Week.

The Empty Quarter is the name of the spring/summer 2011 collection and draws inspiration from the designer's childhood in the Middle East.

What is your favorite work of art?

Richard Serra's sculptures and prints.
They are powerful, masculine and raw.

What is your fetish item of clothing, the one that we see time and time again in your collections?

Key items from spring/summer 2011 would have to be the all-in-one jersey with sailor and oversized hoods. The highlight was the leather jackets with multiple zips.

Kristofer Kongshaug

www.kristoferkongshaug.com

Originally from Norway, Kristofer Kongshaug is the founder and owner of KK, the label that expresses his interests as a fashion designer. He mixes haute couture with a more urban look to create his individual style, marked by anachronism. His first commercial collection, presented in 2008 at the Oslo Fashion Week, won the prize for best collection and best new designer.

Kongshaug is also co-founder of Door Studios Paris, a photography studio, showroom and gallery located in the French capital. The studio serves as a catalyst for designers, photographers and artists who work together.

His designs have attracted the attention of *Elle*, *Marie Claire*, *Vogue* and *WWD*, including other leading names.

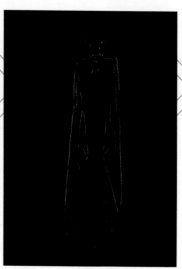

The model Tanya Ruban, the stylist Marcela Acevedo and jewelry designer Ana Carolina Escobar give life to the artistic designs by Kongshaug.

What is your favorite work of art?

A naked female back, the shoulder
blades and the spine creating this
wonderful harmony of outstanding
beauty. When it comes to artworks I
don't really have any favorites, there are
so many great pieces of art. For me its
often just a moment of appreciation,
hence I might like something one day
and hate it the other.

© Elias

What is your fetish item of clothing, the one that we see time and time again in your collections?

For me it must be shirt collars, and my back pleats. It's often these simple things that are the easiest to relate to and build an identity out of.

Ksubi

George Gorrow and Dan Single, Ksubi co-founders, met in Los Angeles in the nineties. Both from Sydney, when they returned to their hometown, they thought it would be fun to work together, and, together with Oska Wright and Paul Wilson, they got down to work. Their first collection consisted of worn jeans torn with garden tools, and the denim was speckled with graphics.

Since then Ksubi grew into a cult label, a lifestyle. Almost like an urban subculture, the label is formed by a group of artists from different disciplines. In the collections, modern punk and teen rebellion come together in a humorous artistic exercise.

www.ksubi.com

The Ksubi hallmark is not only its use of denim, but also the strong personality of its garments: an explosion of attitude.

© Katia Werstar

THIS IS NOT
A BOMB

ksubi

© Matt Reed

What is your favorite work of art?

George Gorrow: My favorite artwork
of my own is an untitled painting of a
girl holding the dagger of death in one
hand and the anti-dollar in the other.

© Rene Vaile

What is your fetish item of clothing, the one that we see time and time again in your collections?

George Gorrow: Other than our jeans, my favorite Ksubi design is a pair of sunglasses "musca" a.k.a. metal flap aviator I did. I liked the simple concept of switching leather for metal.

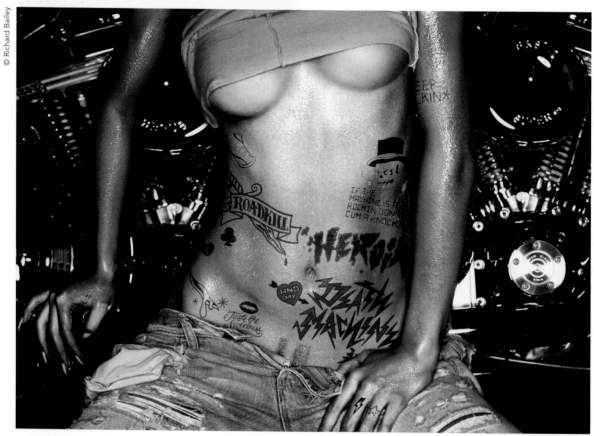

© Richard Bailey

Kumiko Watari

Originally from Osaka (Japan), Kumiko Watari studied at Kyoto City University of Arts. Focusing on textiles, her early work was based on the production of artistic installations, in which she mixed modern techniques with traditional Japanese dying techniques. In 2005, Watari moved to London to study at Central Saint Martins, where she finished perfected her artistic perspective and individual style.

Might-T, her own company, was established in 2007. Her designs combine hand-illustrated prints with a passion for expressiveness, creating garments with a strong personality and sense of humor.

Watari is now based in London, where she combines her work for Might-T with collaborations with other companies as a print designer.

www.kumikowatari.com

To create patterns, Watari can use any item as a starting point, even a plate full of figures made with cream.

Photos by Christopher Dadey

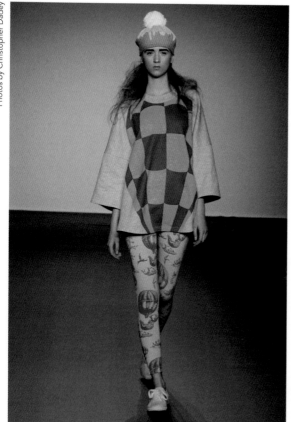

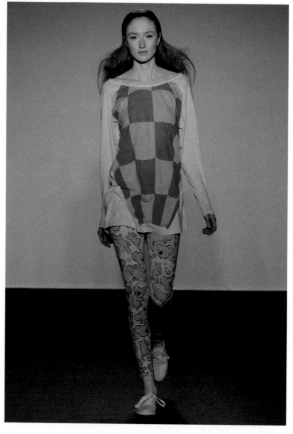

What is your favorite work of art?

Jeff Koons's *Balloon Dog*. I fell in love
when I saw it at a pop art exhibition at
the Boston Museum in 2002.

218 The Poetry of Fashion Design

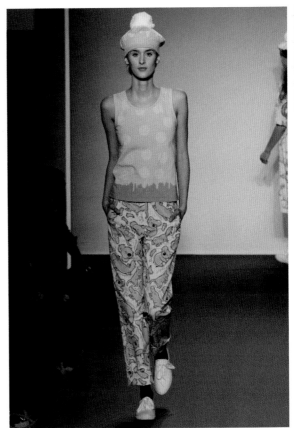

Photos by Christopher Dadey

The Poetry of Fashion Design 219

What is your fetish item of clothing, the one that we see time and time again in your collections?

The doughnut capes and cream face print dress from my autumn/winter 2010 collection. The things that you dreamed when you were a child; I like the idea to make these things come true in fashion.

© Matilde Travassos

One of the skills of Parris is the way to incorporate color in the designs. The geometric shapes are hidden in the fall of the garments.

Lino Villaventura

www.linovillaventura.com.br

Plastic artist and designer, Lino Villaventura is one of the icons of Brazilian fashion design. Since his first appearance on French television in 1987 in a documentary about his country, the designer has grown to become an ambassador for Brazil, exhibiting in Japan, Lebanon, France, Austria and the Netherlands.

The admiration for his work arises from a unique visual enthusiasm, and he has been awarded by the Ministry of Culture, recognizing the positive influence of his work on cultural development.

Villaventura has also collaborated with Mattel and Swarovski, and has participated in movie and theater costume design. His collections are regularly published in magazines such as *Vogue*, *Marie Claire*, *Elle* and *Collezione*.

Op-art from head to toe in the spring/ summer 2011 prints and an obvious artistic heritage throughout the collection.

What is your favorite work of art?

Gustav Klimt, Gustave Moreau,
Friedensreich Hundertwasser, Hiroshi
Sugimoto, Jeff Koons, Hélio Oiticica.
The classics: Botticelli, Ingres, Delacroix,
Goya, Louise Bourgeois.

What is your fetish item of clothing,
the one that we see time and time
again in your collections?

My iconic pieces.

Textures, embroidery and pleats are the designer's leitmotif. Color and movement are the two fundamental elements of this impressive piece.

Louisa Parris

www.louisaparris.com

Upon completing her degree in fashion design and marketing at Central Saint Martins, Louisa Parris launched her design career with internships at DKNY, Mulberry, Gharani Strok and Ghost. Since then she has worked as a freelance designer for labels on both sides of the Atlantic, and in addition to her own collections, she has created costumes for the movies, theater and opera.

Her awards include best female collection from Central Saint Martins and the Gen Art Styles Design Awards in the evening dress category. In addition, her designs have been featured in publications such as *WWD*, *Vogue*, *Zink*, and *The Independent*.

The designer currently lives San Francisco and focuses on elegance, fabrics, color and simplicity.

LOUISA PARRIS

One of the skills
of Parris is the
way to incorporate
color in the designs.
The geometric shapes are
hidden in the fall of the
garments.

What is your favorite work of art?

This is so hard, as I'm discovering new works and appreciating old works all the time.
Ben Nicholson, *March 63 (Artemission)*, 1963
Gruau, *Le Rouge Baiser*, 1949
Robert Doisneau, *La Dernière Valse du 14 Juillett*, 1949
Aubrey Beardsley, *The Peacock Skirt*, illustration for *Salome*, 1894
Jean Loup Sieff, *Maria*, 1959

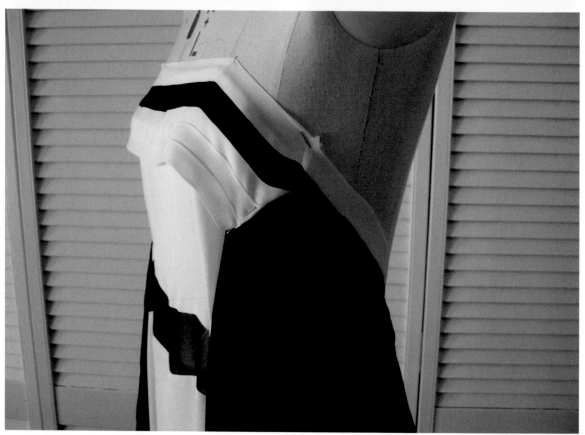

Art Nouveau-inspired, another of the influences that are incorporated into the creations are the graphic compositions by Piet Mondrian.

What is your fetish item of clothing, the one that we see time and time again in your collections?

It changes all the time, and it takes many months for me to appreciate the collection after it has been finished. But at the moment it's the Pauline gown. It has a huge presence and I would love to see it in a grand, modern opera!

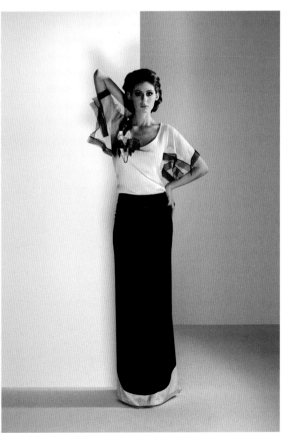

Sober and
ethereal, these
wedding dresses are
a perfect synthesis of
the designer's creative
universe, where elegance
always prevails.

Lucile Puton

lucileputon.net

After finishing her art studies in Besançon (France), Lucile Puton began her training as a textile designer in Paris. There she realized that she was more interested in organic and tangible fashion, and she studied for five years at La Cambre, Belgium. Then, Puton carried out internships at Kris Van Assche, Alexander McQueen and Thom Browne, in New York.

Meanwhile, the designer began to create her own collections for men, which combine an architectural vision of fashion with her knowledge of textiles, coming to show her collection at the prestigious Hyères Festival International.

Currently, the designer is living in Paris, where she continues to develop her career.

The Hide and
Seek collection,
presented in Hyères,
plays with layering,
showing the designer's
skill.

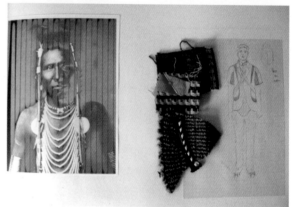

What is your favorite work of art?

It's really difficult to make a choice, 'cause you discover new things all the time. So I'll choose Rothko because I think I will always love his paintings— from the most colorful to the darkest black and grey. For me they are fields of emotions, landscapes for the mind to wander, it's even inspiring. It's one of the rare works of art that I could stare at for hours. And I know it has an influence on the way I see the colors and the materials in my collections. There's also a lot of things I like in art that are related to it, especially about the photography of the sea and the series about cinema theater from Sugimoto. I like when photography stands between abstraction and figuration as well.

© Martin Bing

© Martin Bing

What is your fetish item of clothing, the one that we see time and time again in your collections?

I think especially about the "heavy pieces" in my collections. I always liked working on the jackets/coats, 'cause they need structure, codes, but also because you can work on big volumes and really play with the shape, construct and deconstruct. I like working with heavy materials as well, wool, loden, or even new materials with which you can give structure and "hold" to the garment. I started working on an oversized coat with really round and generous shoulders, but also a graphical game of collars during my fourth year at la Cambre, and I use it as a pattern base for my Hide & Seek collection, transformed into a perfecto anorak. It also gave me the idea for the shape of my trench and for the cape. I think it's a good way to create links in your work.

Maison Martin Margiela

www.maisonmartinmargiela.com

Founded in 1988 by Martin Margiela and Jenny Meirens, la Maison has grown to become a reference point among peers. Exhibitions, stores around the world and the elegant reverence of the fashion industry with its unique personality confirm the recognition of this house that today functions as a group.

Its collections branch into different lines and disciplines, including the design of objects, publications, perfumes and accessories. These include the Artisanal Collection, consisting of handmade items designed using curious materials. In constant evolution, la Maison Martin Margiela is an institution that regenerates itself with each new collection, based on the frontier between design, experimentation and art.

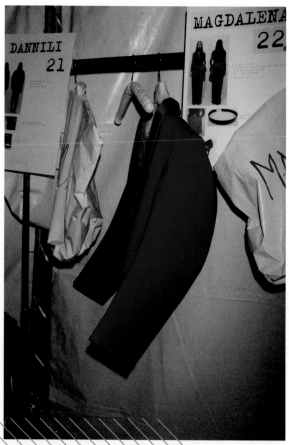

© Andrea Spotorno

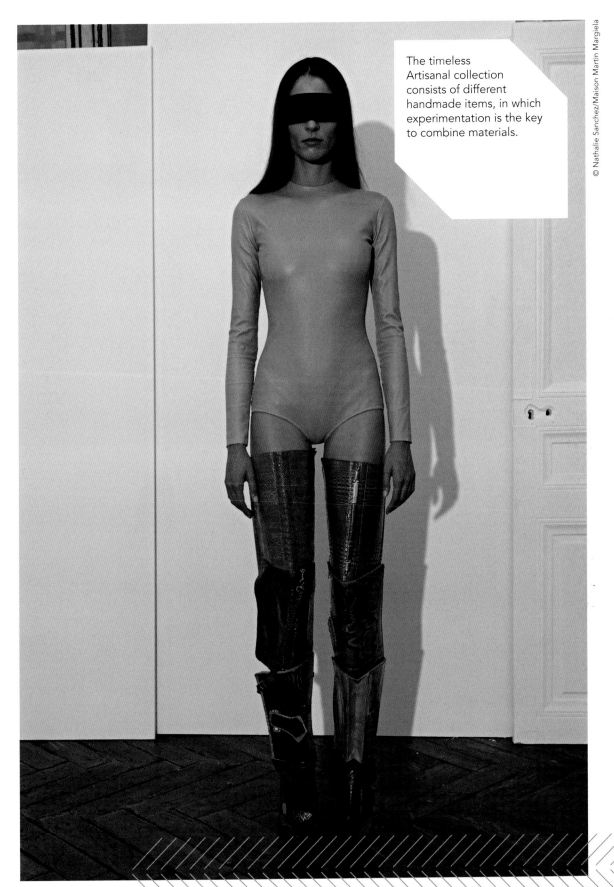

The timeless Artisanal collection consists of different handmade items, in which experimentation is the key to combine materials.

Photos by Nathalie Sanchez/Maison Martin Margiela

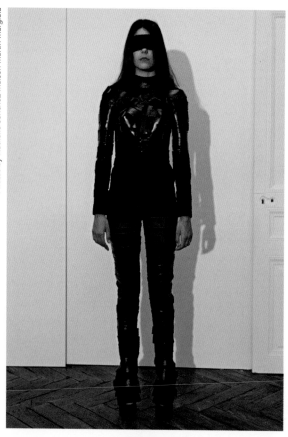

What is your favorite work of art?

All works which are made by artists that insist on confronting the authenticity of their talent. Passion can only merit respect and awe.

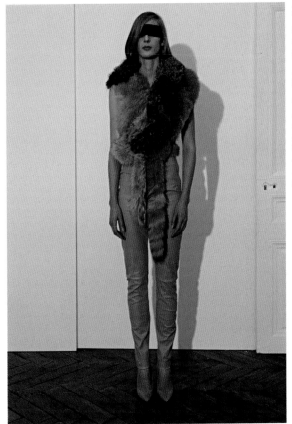

Explosions of red in the backstage of fall/winter 2010/11 runway show collection. This was the color that marked the tone of the season.

Photos by Andrea Spotorno

Photos by Henry Roy

What is your fetish item of clothing, the one that we see time and time again in your collections?

Being a collective, Maison Martin Margiela's answer would be too long.

Photos by Henry Roy

Photos by Giovanni Giannoni/Maison Martin Margiela

Photos by Giovanni Giannoni/Maison Martin Margiela

The collection by this fashion house proposes a waist that does not cling to the body, subverting the natural silhouette.

Mary Wing To

The expertise of leather artist Mary Wing To has become firmly rooted in the equestrian world. Fashion designer turned professional saddler, Wing To studied at the London College of Fashion, garnering fame and recognition due to her individual vision, which includes her two passions: fashion and horses.

Her innovative designs have earned her the prestigious City & Guilds Medal of Excellence Award and, more recently, the Lions Award for creative craftsperson of the year in the UK. She has also won the award for best international designer in the Netherlands and New Zealand for her sculptural creations.

Based in London, Wing To continuously develops her skills with the Royal Mews along with the queens master saddler and harness maker.

www.marywingto.com

Fascinated by horses, the designer takes her inspiration from her extensive experience in the world of saddlery, as can be seen in her sketches.

What is your favorite work of art?

Anatomy of the horse, by George Stubbs.

What is your fetish item of clothing, the one that we see time and time again in your collections?

My work is a complete labor of my "humanhorse" fetish!

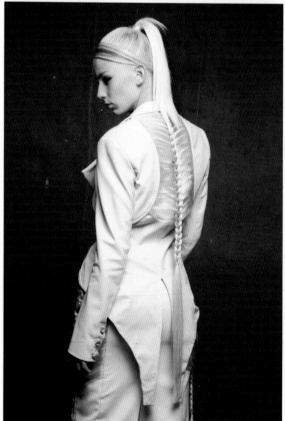

Matohu

The charm of Issey Miyake, Rei Kawakubo and Yohji Yamamoto was what prompted Hiroyuki Horihata and Makiko Sekiguchi, the pair of designers from Matohu, to study fashion at the Bunka Fashion College. After finishing their studies, both carried out their internships as pattern designers. Their experience made them realize there was a huge Western influence in the cuts of most garments, which made them return to their roots. Thus, Matohu was born, the search for common ground between traditional Japanese costumes and the modern world.

The admiration of the beauty of Japanese textures, the perception of empty space in the superimposition of garments and the emphasis on the natural folds of the kimono are the leitmotif of their collections.

www.matohu.com

The proposal
by Matohu relies
on the singularity of
a unique perspective,
mixing traditions, cultures
and modernity.

What is your favorite work of art?

Japanese art and crafts, especially antiques such as Oribe and Shino old pottery.

What is your fetish item of clothing, the one that we see time and time again in your collections?

Nagagi—which is the name and style we created. It is a new category of clothes, neither Western clothes nor kimono, but something beyond them. In every season we make Nagagi with different fabrics and techniques.

Playing with color gradients is based on the Japanese tradition of imitating the natural tones of the different seasons in clothing.

Maxjenny

Maxjenny, an explosion of color and energy, is the brainchild of one of the most exclusive designers on the Scandinavian scene: Maxjenny Forslund. A self-taught fashion designer, Forslund studied furniture design at the Design School of Denmark, and presented his silkscreen furniture, colorful carpets and embroidered sofas in the fairs of Milan, London and New York.

With a renowned reputation behind him, the designer created her first collection in 2007, when she established her own clothing brand. Maxjenny's designs are based on the study of body movement, improvising in line with the possibilities of fabric. Her two lines, The New Black and Streetsculptures, are sold in stores in Denmark, Germany, United Kingdom, China, Italy and Japan.

www.maxjenny.com

© Mads Damgaard

Maxjenny works
with intelligent
materials that can
identify an external
stimulus and respond to it.
Thus, her designs are pure
movement.

Photos by Lars G Svensson

What is your favorite work of art?

Large paintings like Gerhard Richter's. "Warhol after Munch" exhibition—Warhol's *Munch pictures* shown together with several of Munch's original prints, constituting a unique experience and encounter between two great artists. Loads of colors. Neonish. Very white.

What is your fetish item of clothing, the one that we see time and time again in your collections?

The pantone patterns and the pixel patterns. All pictures are named after their pattern. They are my success!

Michael Sontag

This emerging designer on the Berlin fashion scene studied at the National School of Decorative Arts in Paris and the School of Art and Design Berlin-Weissensee. While attending, the designer also did an internship at C.neeon, Frank Leder, Kenzo and Givenchy.

His garments, which are made from natural materials, combine delicacy and femininity in an almost ethereal way, and have attracted the attention of various fashion institutions. Among other awards, Sontag has won the Textile Innovationpreis in 2009 and, more recently, the Start Your Own Business.

The designer, who lives in Berlin, creates each of his garments in his own atelier and presents his collections at the fashion week in the German capital.

© Petrov Ahner

© Christian Schwarzenberg

Asymmetrical and complex forms are the weapons with which Sontag builds, paradoxically, the ethereal impression of his garments.

Photos by Christian Schwarzenberg

What is your favorite work of art?

Marina Abramovic's *Rhythm 0.*

Photos by Christian Schwarzenberg

What is your fetish item of clothing, the one that we see time and time again in your collections?

A draped white wool-silk pantsuit with white shirt.

Miriam Ponsa

www.miriamponsa.com

Miriam Ponsa graduated in design from the University of Southampton and later specialized in design and knitting techniques in Igualada. Her work is recognized for its delicate pattern design and fabrics, which are dyed with exclusive silk-screen printing.

The Catalan designer is committed to innovation without fear. In addition to her normal line, she has created the Miriam Ponsa Laboratory, where she experiments with latex and other unusual materials in tailoring. The handmade pieces created in the laboratory are unique and limited; they are exclusively presented in her runway shows.

Her collections are available in Spain, France, Belgium, Italy, Denmark, Norway, Russia, Japan, USA and Saudi Arabia.

The fall/winter 2010/11 collection is entitled Textura Social and is inspired by nomadic cultures that use traditional techniques in their fabrics.

What is your favorite work of art?

It is impossible to choose one. I love land art. I love Andy Goldsworthy, in painting I love Van Gogh, and architecture, Gaudí and Zaha Hadid.

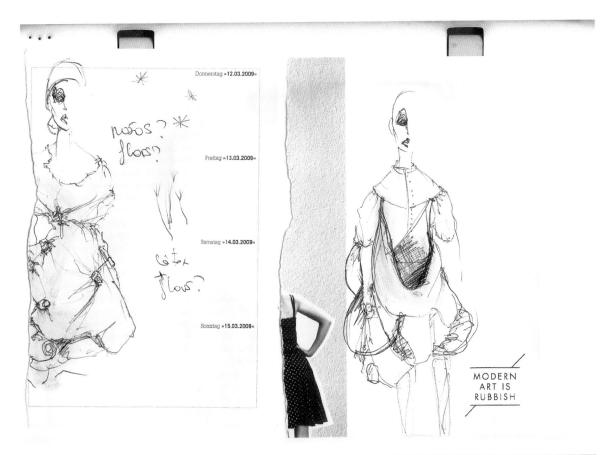

MODERN
ART IS
RUBBISH

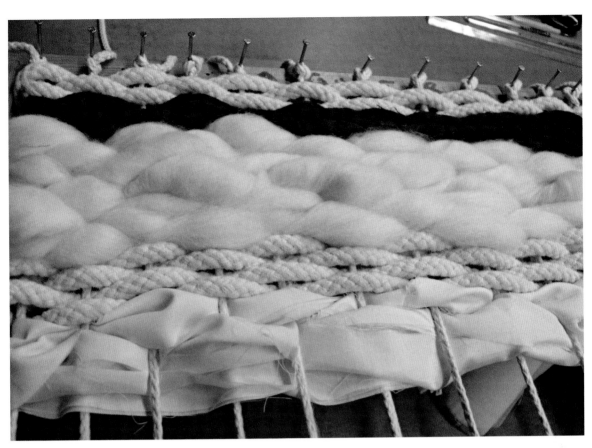

Mixing ancient
and contemporary
cultures, the knitted
garments are handled
like living things that are
constantly changing.

What is your fetish item of clothing, the one that we see time and time again in your collections?

An unstructured jacket with many irregular folds in plush.

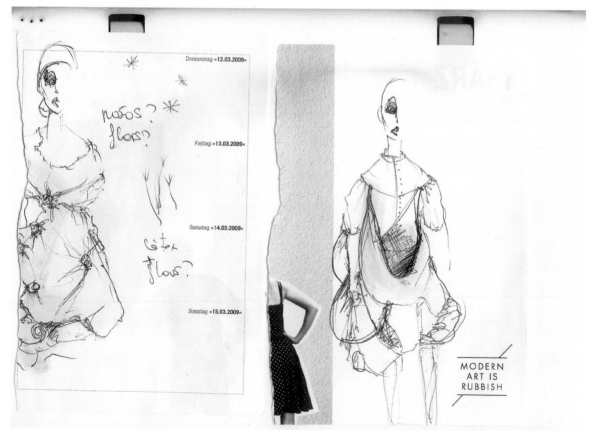

Wide and overlapping forms, the accessories symbolize the journey and load, inspired by the Himalayan people.

Moi Multiple

A former student of astrophysics, Anna Francesca Ceccon studied fashion at the Istituto Europeo di Design. Her first steps into the world of fashion were as coolhunter, but it did not take her very long to show her unique talent as a designer, when in 2008 she launched her own brand, Moi Multiple.

Ceccon, worldly wise and a lover of storytelling, conceives each collection as a different story, but with a common concept that links them: the prismatic individual that multiplies into thousands. Hence the name of the label, which creates a wardrobe for a modern woman who has different roles in modern life. Between the movement and structure, her clothes play with color, irony and surprising details.

www.moimultiple.com

The spring/ summer 2010 Lègami-Legàmi collection demonstrates Ana Ceccon's ability to use materials in storytelling.

What is your favorite work of art?

It is difficult for me to focus on just one work of art, I like all the Giacomo Balla pieces—his dynamic movement and fixed dynamism. Also the works of Schiele and Klimt have a special place in my heart.

What is your fetish item of clothing, the one that we see time and time again in your collections?

I would say corsetry, as in the sublimation of the structural lines around the body.

The fall/winter 2010/11 collection shows the transient nature of Moi Multiple styles: Mood swings so as not to be pigeonholed.

Natsumi Zama

www.natsumizama.com

Currently residing in London, Natsumi Zama studied fashion design at the Bunka Fashion College, and continued her studies in fashion design and technology, specializing in women's collections at the London College of Fashion. During her training she worked as an assistant to Louise Goldin and when she finished her studies, she worked as a machinist in Future Classics. Finally, she launched her own label in 2010.

Natsumi Zama's style is based on minimalist, chic and pure tailoring. The collection she presented at her graduation was exhibited in an exclusive show for the press in London, and was inspired by the kimono. With huge bows arranged in different ways, the monochrome palette of the garments defined her purist aesthetic and outlined the details.

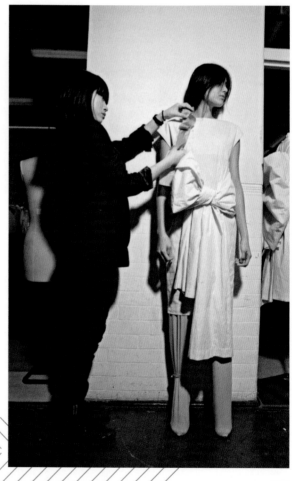

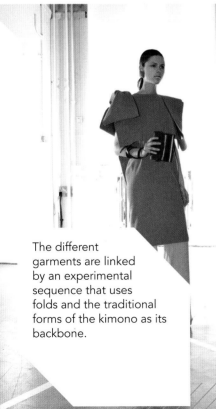

The different garments are linked by an experimental sequence that uses folds and the traditional forms of the kimono as its backbone.

What is your favorite work of art?

I don't have a great knowledge of
art, but I'm interested in Art Deco.
I'm always fascinated by the interior,
products and fashion of that era. They
have both beauty in their shape and
functionality as products, yet they are
formed by simple lines.

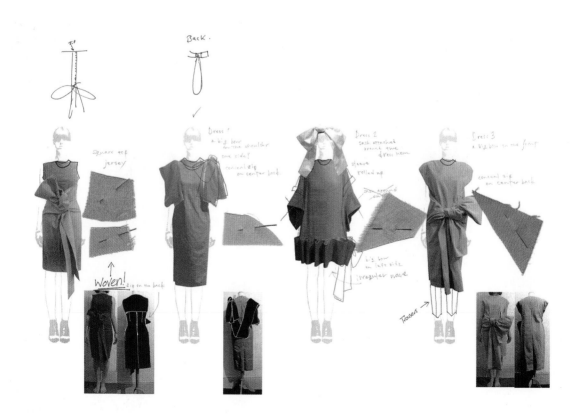

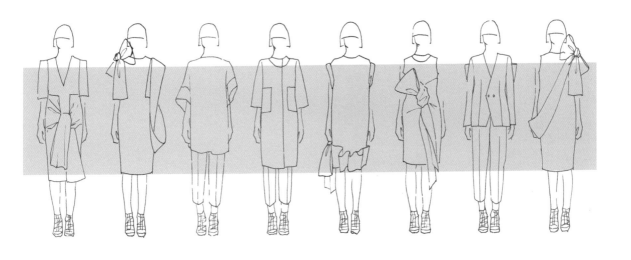

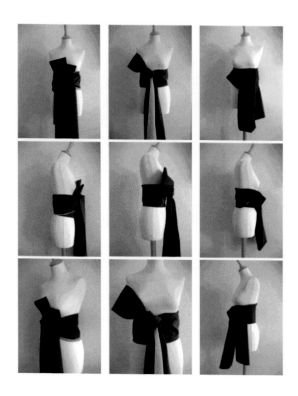

What is your fetish item of clothing, the one that we see time and time again in your collections?

It is difficult to choose… but I would say that the dress with obi on the front and the wool coat with obi on the back are my favorites. I like the design, which is simple but unique. These two garments have long bows and wearers can arrange them as they like by folding, tying, or maybe hanging them on their shoulders. The design is composed of a simple structure, but the simplicity can be its uniqueness.

Potipoti

www.potipoti.com

©Ramiro E.

Potipoti is the brainchild of the designers Silvia Salvador and Nando Cornejo.

Spanish by birth and currently living in Berlin, they began their project in 2005 after working with several Spanish studios. Their distinctive aesthetic is the result of their unique vision of graphic design, which they successfully convey in the world of fashion. Their collections, which show their skill in knitwear, are designed in Berlin and then manufactured in small family businesses in Castilla y León.

In recent years, their creations have been presented on the most famous runways, such as El Ego de Cibeles, the Mustang Fashion Weekend, Pictoplasma and Pasarela Abierta. Apart from their own store in Berlin, their designs can be found in Sweden, Japan, Germany, Denmark, France and Spain.

Photos by Frank Kalero

The incorporation of patterns and prints is the definitive hallmark of Potipoti and where their graphic experience is reflected.

What is your favorite work of art?

The circus, by Alexander Calder.

Photos by ©Jose Salas & Xavi Bove

What is your fetish item of clothing, the one that we see time and time again in your collections?

A mohair poncho for winter.

Robert Geller

Born in Hamburg (Germany), Robert Geller developed an early interest in design, which led him to study at the Rhode Island School of Design. Geller complemented his studies with an internship at Marc Jacobs, helping to create four men's collections. He moved to Cloak, where he developed the visual aesthetics, which he would later apply to his own designs. His work, along with Alexandre Plokhov's work for this label earned him several awards, including the Ecco Domani Fashion Foundation's in 2003.

In 2006, Geller founded his own label and his work earned him recognition as one of the new up-and-coming talents in the U.S. men's fashion scene. Today, his garments, produced in Japan, are sold in more than fifty stores worldwide.

www.robertgeller-ny.com

© Thomas Lohr

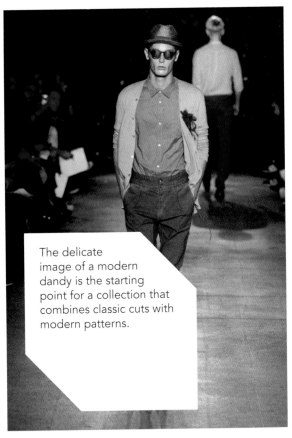

The delicate image of a modern dandy is the starting point for a collection that combines classic cuts with modern patterns.

What is your favorite work of art?

I have a portrait of my mother done by
Andy Warhol. They were quite friendly
and this captures her youth really
beautifully.

What is your fetish item of clothing, the one that we see time and time again in your collections?

It would be our leather jackets. We have them in every collection and they are always our stand-out pieces. Through washes, detailing and hardware we really create something special.

Roberta Furnaletto

Roberta Furnaletto is motivated by a fierce need for self-expression and her work is the result of curiosity and a never-ending desire to experiment. After graduating from the Academy of Fine Arts in Milan, her transition into the world of fashion was when Christian Lacroix was shown a piece of her artwork. He liked it so much that he invited her to collaborate with him. She created exclusive pieces for the Lacroix haute couture runway shows and moved on to collaborate with Dior, Ungaro and Azzedine Alaïa.

Each piece is created, developed and constructed on the body in her delicate collections, basing her designs on volume, symmetry and contrast. Suspended between geometry and pattern design, her designs are the realization of an idea that is both artistic and technical, reproducing its emotional intensity.

www.robertafurlanetto.com

This dress from the spring/summer 2010 collection is a favorite of Furnaletto. Its folds and layers are reminiscent of the sea, hence its name, Sea Anemona.

What is your favorite work of art?

Gustave Moreau's *The Apparition*.

What is your fetish item of clothing, the one that we see time and time again in your collections?

The Diaspro dress Sophia of the autumn/winter 2010/11 collection.

The designer
works with puffed
garments, in which
volumes are sustained
invisibly and display a
flawless technique.

Saara Lepokorpi

www.saaralepokorpi.com

A designer and pattern designer since 2002, Saara Lepokorpi completed her studies at the University of Art and Design in Helsinki in 2009. Her work blends subtlety with fierce modernity, alternating handcrafted pieces with others made using industrial techniques. The result is a delicate but transgressive style, in which the patterns are mixed with an in-depth knowledge of the many possibilities of textiles.

Her creations with organic materials have earned a Copenhagen Fashion Summit Award, an award which rewards sustainable fashion, and her designs have reached France, Spain and the U.K. Named young designer of the year 2007 in Finland, her artistic perspective of the world of fashion was recognized by the Arts Council of Finland in 2010.

The fall/winter 2010/11 collection is a fantasy that combines color stains with white puristy: punk delicacy.

What is your favorite work of art?

I watch lots of movies. One I was left positively haunted by is *Sud Pralad*, by director Apichatpong Weerasethakul. Usually I'm inclined to make some sort of interpretation seeing a movie, but this one didn't seem to have so much analytical content. Instead it delivered a strong feeling, unrelated to the film's events as such, and unique from what I've experienced before. I was completely immersed in the film's world, and at the end of the film a single frame triggered the flow of emotion that washed over me. Everything before that seemed to be just preparation for that single event. I have huge respect for anyone who can put me through such an experience.

© Liisa Valonen

The designer
also teaches
fashion illustration.
By comparing her
sketches and designs one
can see the realism of her
drawings.

What is your fetish item of clothing, the one that we see time and time again in your collections?

I'm very inclined to designing dresses. In a dress I find it easiest to incorporate everything essential about my design esthetic. Perhaps it's because a dress can be seen as a complete outfit. And perhaps I'm slightly control-freakish... so I like being able to create the whole look in one go. Someone might say I'm a designer for cocktail dresses, but I like to think of people wearing my dresses for everyday situations as well. No matter how fancy a dress is—as long as it's not a long gown—one can always create an everyday look around it.

Photos by Liisa Valonen

Lepokorpi's experience as a stylist can be seen in the presentation of the collection, because the accessories and finishes complement the garments.

Toga

www.toga.jp

This label, which takes its name from ancient Greek attire, is the brainchild of Yasuko Furuta, who founded the label in 1997, having completed her studies in Paris ESMOD. Distinguished by its unique fabrics and volumes, Toga's proposed style is urban, cutting edge, and profoundly contemporary.

Toga caught the attention of buyers and fashion journalists after its first individual runway show in 2001 during Tokyo Fashion Week. Two years later, Furuta won the Mainichi Fashion Award for her fall/winter 2003/2004 collection, and soon after she opened her first store in Tokyo. Toga is now sold in more than thirty stores worldwide.

In the Waveform collection, movement is expressed through the pleats, fringes, the gathers and drapes.

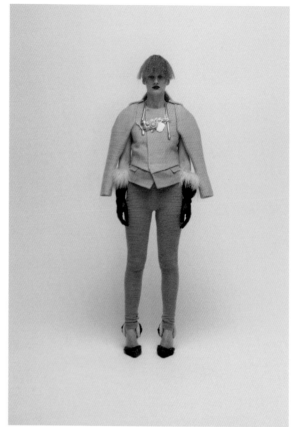

What is your favorite work of art?

I like works and authors who give the chance to change perspective in daily life. Jeremy Deller is an artist that I'm very curious about right now.

What is your fetish item of clothing, the one that we see time and time again in your collections?

When you have a very strong aim or goal, it can limit your range of creativity. So I try not to be a slave to previous knowledge and experiences, and instead try to learn and bring in new things that happen in the creative process.

Besides the work of pattern design, the personality of the collection is also built from the combination of textures and prints.

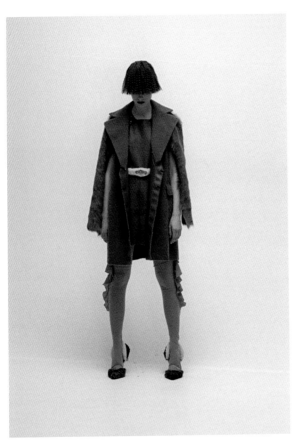

Txell Miras

www.txellmiras.eu

In the world there are some people who have a creative mind, so they cannot stop thinking, imagining. If this is added to a genuine interest in the multiple ways and supports of expression, then perhaps this forms a complete artist who is constantly creating because they do not know otherwise. Without a doubt, one of those people is the indefatigable Txell Miras.

Her background in fine arts and fashion are the focus of Miras work in the shape of the human body and conceptual art, inspired by film, literature, music and artistic expression in general. Thus, her collections are a facet of her many interests, including illustration, painting, photo montages and creating objects with a Dadaist air.

© Hugo de la Rosa

In her fall-winter 2010-2011 collection, called Fancy Bats, Miras reinterprets the many positions of a bat.

What is your favorite work of art?

It's difficult to choose just one. More so than one individual piece of art I'm interested in the works of art covering the career of artists. My favorite artists for many years now have been: Duchamp, Boltanski, Beuys, Kiki Smith, Dreyer, Bergman and Kafka, among others.

Photo by Josep Capdevila

In the Framing collection, the designer shows a sense of humor with the squares and references the act of framing.

What is your fetish item of clothing, the one that we see time and time again in your collections?

A half skirt I made a few years is very dear to me and I have made several variations of it to create a piece that is half skirt and half trousers. This pretty much sums up my obsessions in the creation process. Masculinity against femininity, pattern design against draping, volume against silhouette, stiffness against volatility... In each collection, I have my favorite pieces, it's difficult to choose.

© Josep Capdevila

Ute Ploier

www.uteploier.com

After her time at Central Saint Martins, where she studied fashion and graphic design, Ute Ploier continued her studies at the University of Applied Arts in Vienna. Experience with Jean-Charles de Castelbajac, Viktor & Rolf and Raf Simons led her to present her first collection in 2000, while still in college.

Ten years later, Ute Ploier is a designer with a label going by the same name. Humor, irony and an entertaining transgression of playing with established social roles can be identified in her collections. The idea of masculinity is constructed and deconstructed in her clothes and campaigns, challenging dress codes and putting social labels at risk. The unusual fabric combinations are just the icing on the cake.

© Martin Stöbich

© Guenter Parth

The lookbook images by Man Machine play with the concept of the collection's name, forcing the garments into humorous positions.

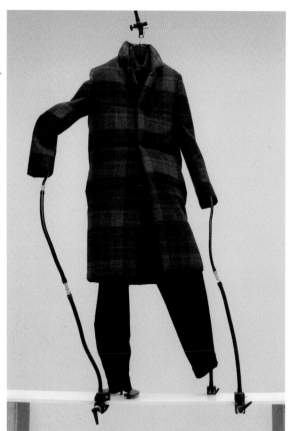

What is your favorite work of art?

The Cremaster Cycle, by Matthew Barney.

What is your fetish item of clothing, the one that we see time and time again in your collections?

A waxed, caramel-colored trench coat.

The collection
Ute Ploier 8.5, for
spring/summer 2010,
offers a retro look.

Vladimir Karaleev

Born and raised in Sofia (Bulgaria), Vladimir Karaleev moved to Berlin to study fashion at the University of Applied Sciences. In 2005, he founded his own company and launched his first collection, Cut 210, in which the qualities that still characterize him could be seen.

The innovative silhouettes and experimental cuts are the mainstays of the designer's creations. Modern art has a great influence on his work, and the close bond that unites it with the art scene is not only expressed through his conceptual approach but also through his runway shows.

In 2010, he won the third prize in the Start Your Own Business. Since then, Karaleev has worked as a lecturer at the University of Applied Sciences.

As if origami structures, the garments in the Pro Forma collection are folded with an unusual autonomy.

Photos by Jonas Lindström

What is your favorite work of art?

Isa Genzken, *Ground Zero* series.
Jenny Holzer, *Protect me from what
I want*
Anish Kapoor, *Memory*
Mark Rothko, *Red, Black (untitled)*

What is your fetish item of clothing, the one that we see time and time again in your collections?

3T dress, from my first collection, a dress made from three T-shirts; Blue filz dress, from the Pro Forma collection.

© Jonas Lindström

Walter Van Beirendonck

www.waltervanbeirendonck.com

Walter Van Beirendonck shot to international fame as one of the Antwerp Six and he has never neglected the impertinent genius that characterizes him. Versatile, Van Beirendonck is not only one of the male designers with the most power to influence the fashion industry, but also he is a curator, book illustrator and a fundamental member of creative think tanks.

Art, music, literature, nature and ethnicity synchronously officiate in each of his collections, which stand out for their powerful graphics and surprising color combinations. In addition, his individual views on society accompany his shows as slogans displayed in unconventional contexts.

© Dan Lecca

Take a W-ride is a military-inspired collection from a recreational perspective. Planes and guns are part of the prints.

Photos by Dan Lecca

What is your favorite work of art?

Tomato Head, by Paul McCarthy.

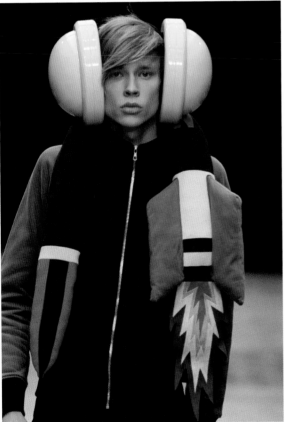

What is your fetish item of clothing, the one that we see time and time again in your collections?

The masks I've created since I started making collections. I love the effect and the impact they have on the person wearing it.

Photos by Dan Lecca

The juxtapositions of patterns and colors are not only key for Read My Skin, but also an element that is ever-present in the designer's work.

Yiorgos Eleftheriades

www.yiorgoseleftheriades.gr

Yiorgos Eleftheriades, with 40 collections for women and 22 for men behind him, has presented his designs in Athens, Paris, London and Barcelona. His philosophy is based on his interest in classical forms, seeking contemporary elegance. Thus, the Greek designer attempts to create an alternative urban style with interesting shapes, strong tailoring and combinations of different fabrics and textures. The contrast of elements is another of his trademarks, and several leitmotifs can be identified in his designs: the high tech and retro, the masculine and feminine, the luxurious and functional.

His collections have been published in *Numéro*, *Vogue*, *Harper's Bazaar*, *Zoo Magazine*, *iD* and *Glamour*, among others.

Movement, technology, delicacy, femininity, experimentation: the designer's long career supports his fascinating ability for self-improvement.

What is your favorite work of art?

Pollock's painting is one of my favorites. Gaudí's architecture—work of art and Edward Weston's black-and-white photos.

What is your fetish item of clothing, the one that we see time and time again in your collections?

The part of the tailoring pieces of each collection.

Yong Kyun Shin

www.yongkyunshin.com

The son of a jewelry designer, Yong Kyun Shin grew up in the fashion world. After studying fine arts in his native South Korea, he continued his training as a pattern designer and then he studied fashion design at Central Saint Martins. His resumé includes an internship with Alexander McQueen, where under the watchful eye of Sarah Burton he took charge of most of the illustrations in the female collections. He has also worked in the Viktor & Rolf studios.

His graduate collection, presented in 2010, has surprised critics and industry personalities. Based on op-art, his clothes mix wool, cashmere and leather, and show a great ability to generate three-dimensional shapes.

Currently in London, Shin plans to continue his studies at Central Saint Martins.

Future designer-
artist and master
of the unusual, Yong
Kyun Shin's sketches are
complete pieces of work
and just as surprising as his
clothing.

What is your favorite work of art?

Zdzislaw Beksinski's painting.
Vincent van Gogh's *Sunflowers*.

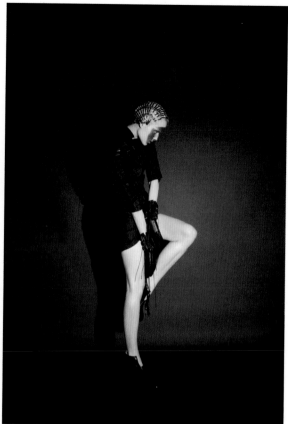

What is your fetish item of clothing, the one that we see time and time again in your collections?

My favorite piece could be the black leather jacket with dress. It took longer than any other piece and it shows a lot of things that I want to say. Connected little details show the great outline of the jacket and the very tight body-conscious dress shows the beautiful human body. Overall, I think the whole piece is well balanced and delivers perfect harmony with the body and the cloth.

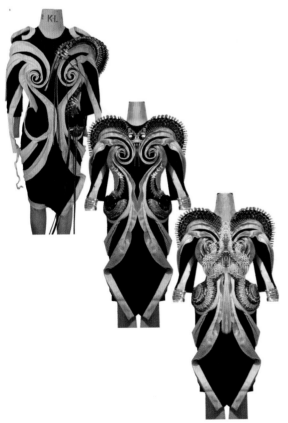

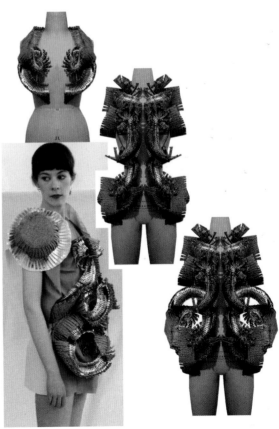

The piece in this photo is the one that the designer earned a special prize for in the ITS#NINE competition sponsored by Diesel.